how i discovered poetry

marilyn nelson

illustrations by Hadley Hooper

Dial Books

an imprint of Penguin Group (USA) LLC

DIAL BOOKS
Published by the Penguin Group
Penguin Group (USA) LLC
375 Hudson Street
New York, New York 10014

USA/Canada/UK/Ireland/Australia/New Zealand/India/South Africa/China
penguin.com
A Penguin Random House Company

Library of Congress Cataloging-in-Publication Data
Nelson, Marilyn, date, author.
[Poems. Selections]
How I discovered poetry / Marilyn Nelson ; illustrations by Hadley Hooper.
pages cm
ISBN 978-0-8037-3304-6 (hardcover : alk. paper)
1. Nelson, Marilyn, date—Poetry. 2. Authorship—Poetry.
3. Poetry—Authorship. I. Hooper, Hadley, illustrator. II. Title.
PS35   2013005289

Manufactured in China on acid-free paper
1 3 5 7 9 10 8 6 4 2
Designed by Lily Malcom
Text set in Garamond

To my corporeal and soul siblings, Jennifer and Mel,

and to my other sisters and brothers

—M.N.

how i
discovered
poetry

Blue Footsies

(Cleveland, Ohio, 1950)

Once upon a time. Upon a time?
Something got on a time? What is a time?
When it got on a time, could it get off?
Could it get on a time two times? Three times?
Three times upon a time . . . Times on a time . . .
Three times on time . . . Or three times on three times . . .
I hear Jennifer's breath. Our room is dark.
Mama's voice questions and Daddy's answers,
a sound seesaw through the wall between us.
If there was, once upon a time, a fire,
and I could only rescue one of them,
would I save him, or her? Or Jennifer?
Four-year-old saves three people from hot flames!
God bless Mama, Daddy, and Jennifer . . .

Church

(Cleveland, Ohio, 1950)

Why did Lot have to take his wife and flea
from the bad city, like that angel said?
Poor Lot: imagine having a pet flea.
I'd keep mine on a dog. But maybe fleas
were bigger in the olden Bible days.
Maybe a flea was bigger than a dog,
more like a sheep or a goat. Maybe they had
flea farms back then, with herds of giant fleas.
Jennifer squirms beside me on the pew,
sucking her thumb, nestled against Mama.
Maybe Lot and his wife rode saddled fleas!
Or drove a coach pulled by a team of fleas!
I giggle soundlessly, but Mama swats
my leg, holding a finger to her lips.

Called Up

(Cleveland, Ohio, 1951)

Folding the letter and laying it down,
Daddy says, "Well, Baby, I've been called back up."
Mama pauses, then puts my bowl of beans
in front of me. Jennifer eats and hums
across from me on two telephone books.
Mama says, "Pray God you won't see combat."
Jennifer, stop singing at the table,
I hiss. Her humming's driving me crazy.
She looks up from her bowl with dreaming eyes:
Huh? Mama says, "My darling, we're going, too."
Stop singing! "I'll take a leave from law school,"
he says, "and you'll take a leave from your job."
We've been called up. Our leaves become feathers.
With wings we wave good-bye to our cousins.

Texas Protection

(James Connally AFB, Texas, 1951)

America goes on and on and on and on,
and on the land are cities, towns, and roads
that stream under your wheels like stripy snakes
and end up in Texas, with new people.
Our dog, Pudgy, found a new family.
Mayflower School feels like something I dreamed
before I woke up wanting cowboy boots
and craving the cap pistol's puff of smoke.
Mama says, "We're walking on eggshells here."
Daddy returns the faceless men's salutes.
But I would tiptoe in my cowboy boots,
I promise, without breaking any eggs!
And if I had a gun and a holster
I could protect us from the Communists!

Telling Time

(James Connally AFB, Texas, 1951)

Mama reminds me I'm a big girl now:
I'm five years old. I can watch Jennifer
for five minutes; they'll just be down the street.
They tuck us in. I hear the door lock click.
Five minutes. "Just five minutes," Daddy said.
My first-grade class is learning to read clocks,
so I know minutes are the little lines
between numbers. Clocks are how you tell time.
Past is before now; future is after.
Now is a five-minute eternity,
Jennifer and I howling in pajamas
in the front yard of the housing unit,
surrounded by concerned faceless strangers
who back away, now our parents are here.

Bomb Drill

(Lackland AFB, Texas, 1952)

Nothing belongs to us in our new house
except Mama's piano and our clothes.
I'm the new girl in *Dick and Jane* country,
the other children faceless as grown-ups.
I read through recess and take some books home.
I read to Jennifer while Mama plays.
I read while the television talker
talks about *career* and the *hide drajen bomb*.
Mama says she's going to vote for Ike.
Daddy says, *"Woman, you just think he's cute!"*
We ducked and covered underneath our desks,
hiding from drajen bombs in school today.
Maybe drajens would turn into butter
if they ran really fast around a tree.

Pink Menace

(Lackland AFB, Texas, 1952)

The Bomb Drill bell is not the Fire Drill bell
or the Tornado bell or the Recess
bell or the bell that says Time to Go Home.
Everybody's motto is Be Prepared,
so we practice Tragic Catastrophes,
hoping they won't come. (*Keep your fingers crossed.*)
My many secret good-luck rituals
seem to be working okay. (*Knock on wood.*)
I never step on cracks in the sidewalk:
America's safe from The Red Menace.
I touch a finger to the car window
whenever we drive over railroad tracks:
the Menace turns pink and fuzzy. At night,
I'm asleep before the end of my blessing list.

A Snake

(Lowry AFB, Colorado, 1953)

As soon as we got here, we turned around
and drove back through the no-guardrail mountains,
connecting the dots of farm mailboxes
to towns and faceless people who don't count.
Mama hugged Aunt Carma and Uncle George.
Daddy wiped his tears with his handkerchief.
Oneida wasn't in her pink bedroom.
She wasn't in the hospital, either.
They said she was in that box. She was dead.
We drove back through the frightening mountains.
Jennifer and I chanted *There's a snake!*
to keep ourselves from looking at the huge
and scaredy-fying emptiness.
When you die, you go to a different school.

Your Own

(Smoky Hill AFB, Kansas, 1953)

Our new house, Officers' Quarters 42,
connects to other quarters and mowed yards
connecting to wheat fields and wilderness
waiting to be explored by kids and dogs.
Sometimes we don't come in until we're called
by someone's mom. They say *Mom,* not *Mama.*
Hazel, Charlotte, Jeannie, Tommy, and Charles:
as soon as we hear the School's Over bell
we flock together like migrating birds,
catching grasshoppers, gathering bouquets,
or just plain running into breathlessness.
I don't know why Mama looked sad tonight
while I was washing up, or why she said,
"Be careful: Don't like them more than your own."

Bad Name

(Smoky Hill AFB, Kansas, 1954)

The dishes washed and dried, my homework done,
and *Amos 'n' Andy* still an hour away,
I kneel with crayons at the coffee table,
drawing and coloring. Round head, round eyes,
half-circle eyebrows, and half-circle mouths.
Segregation means people are kept apart
and *integration* means they're together.
TV is black-and-white, but people aren't.
There's a bad name mean people might call you,
but words aren't sticks and stones. At school today,
James told Mrs. Liebel he didn't say
that name at me. He said he said, "Don't be
a *noogie-hitter*." That's when you just poke
the tetherball instead of punching it.

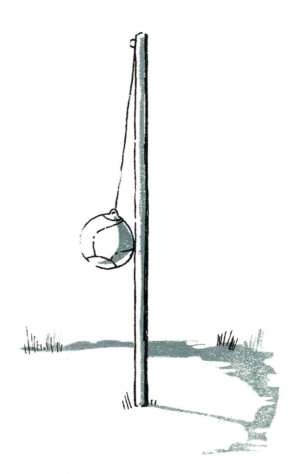

Sonic Boom

(Smoky Hill AFB, Kansas, 1954)

My best friend's name is Tommy Avery.
His mom talks funny because she's English.
They have a little toy Winston Churchill
that puffs real smoke when she lights its cigar.
She made Tommy's fancy birthday dinner
from a recipe in a magazine:
Fiesta Peach Spam Loaf with canned string beans.
Eight candles on his chocolate birthday cake.
Lieutenant Avery was in uniform
and Tommy was wearing his Cub Scout neckerchief.
His mom said, "We can all sleep well at night,
safeguarded by such good-looking soldiers."
While we were singing, a jet made a sonic boom,
like a hammer on an iron curtain.

Career Girl

(Smoky Hill AFB, Kansas, 1954)

Mama's what people call a "career girl."
That's a mother that doesn't stay at home.
She teaches second grade in the base school.
Her all-white class may be a Negro First.
School days start when she zips on her girdle
and calls, "Good morning, chickadees, rise and shine!"
We race to get dressed. Mama braids our hair
as we spoon our cornflakes. The other moms
cook scrambled eggs, pack their kids' lunch boxes
with crustless sandwiches and homemade treats.
They don't shoo their kids out of the kitchen.
They don't frown over red-penciled papers.
They don't say they're too busy for checkers.
They don't care about Making History.

Making History

(Smoky Hill AFB, Kansas, 1955)

Somebody took a picture of a class
standing in line to get polio shots
and published it in the *Weekly Reader.*
We stood like that today. And it did hurt.
Mrs. Liebel said we were Making History,
but all I did was sqwunch up my eyes and wince.
Making History takes more than standing in line
believing little white lies about pain.
Mama says First Negroes are History:
First Negro Telephone Operator,
First Negro Opera Singer at the Met,
First Negro Pilots, First Supreme Court Judge.
That lady in Montgomery just became a First
by sqwunching up her eyes and sitting there.

Gold Box

(Smoky Hill AFB, Kansas, 1955)

I list things I'd take to a bomb shelter
if we had a bomb shelter, which we don't,
so why would I keep working on my list
except because it holds the things I love
so tightly in my mind, they can't fall out?
I keep the list in my gold fruitcake tin.
Jennifer has one for her treasures, too.
I'd take my gold box to a bomb shelter,
but we don't have one. Nobody we know
has a bomb shelter. But they still make bombs.
There's TV talk about them every night
before the good shows come on, and I laugh
at *I Love Lucy* and *Sergeant Bilko*
or lose myself in *The Ed Sullivan Shew.*

Kemo Sabe

(Smoky Hill AFB, Kansas, 1955)

We're watching *The Lone Ranger* on TV.
I'd like to marry Tonto when I grow up:
He's so handsome. I love how he says *how*.

Mama grew up in Indian Country.
"Your grandmother taught in a Creek-Seminole school,"
she says. *Blah, blah . . .* "As a matter of fact,
for a while in high school, a Creek boy was sweet on me."

Daddy says, "Lucky you got out of there
and met me! Marilyn, you could have been
named Pocahontas!"
                            The room disappears.
A me with another name? An Indian me?
Could I be someone else, but think my thoughts?
How different could I be, and still be me?
The music throbs. They ride toward the sunset.

Mississippi

(Smoky Hill AFB, Kansas, 1955)

Over the river and through the woods, for miles
of four-lane highways, slowed by blowing snow,
through towns named for long-vanquished Indians,
to Aunt Charlie's house in Omaha we go.
Hypnotized by the rhythm of tire chains,
I eat a sandwich passed from the front seat,
where Mama and Daddy are talking about a boy
named Emmett. Jennifer, whispering to her doll,
crosses the line between her side and mine,
and when I poke her just a little bit,
she howls as if it hurts, out of sheer spite.
"BEHAVE!"
Lost again in the inwardness of thought
and my five senses, I add to my list:
Thank you for not stationing us in Mississippi.

Glow-in-the-Dark

(Smoky Hill AFB, Kansas, 1956)

Some TV Negroes have shine-in-the-dark
white eyes and teeth and are afraid of ghosts.
I slip out of my twin bed, tiptoe to
our dresser mirror, and grin in the dark.
To my relief, my teeth and eyes don't shine.
In the no-lights-on-at-midnight mirror,
I'm a darker outline against darkness.
Behind my silhouette, my Sunday School
Attendance Award cross is still glowing
in the shadowed cubicle of my headboard,
between my gold plastic music box clock
and my gold fruitcake tin full of treasures.
Guided by its dying phosphorescence,
I slide back into my warm blanket nest.

Traveling Light

(Smoky Hill AFB, Kansas, 1956)

In memory, Pudgy is just a tail
brushing my thighs as we surveyed the shelves
in the icebox. "Pudgy," Daddy explained,
"went to live with a different family;
she's fed and happy." Lady welcomed us
to one Officers Housing, where she lived
under our unit. She was a good dog.
She seemed almost sad when we drove away
behind the moving van. And General
did have a knack for causing us trouble:
He dug up gardens, dragged whole clotheslines home.
"He'll be happier with his new family,"
Daddy explains. We've been transferred again.
We stand numb as he gives away our toys.

Just Pick a Name

(On the Road, 1956)

The miles enter my eyes and disappear
like cigarette smoke from the car window.
The sky seems to be bigger in the West.
I'm growing bigger inside to take it in.
The landscape feeds my hungry eyes a feast
beyond imagining. Who lived before
in places streaming past like scenery?
What if I left a note in a mailbox
out in the boonies, far from any town,
that said, *I know it's hard. You're doing fine.*
I wonder: Would that make things different?
You could just pick a name from the phone book
of any of these bypassed Podunk towns
and send a postcard signed, *Be happy. God.*

Say It

(Mather AFB, California, 1956)

Base Housing is a little ranch house town
with smooth sidewalks perfect for roller skates.
I'm the best reader in Mrs. Krull's class.
Helene's parents are Mama and Daddy's friends
from way back when both men were cadets;
now they're the only Negro officers
on base. But there are two here, not just one.
Helene's a year ahead of me in school.
She's going to be a nurse when she grows up.
We were strolling in the NCO neighborhood
today, when a blond girl jeered from her yard
that she could say a word that would make us mad.
Helene said, "Say it." And when the girl did,
Helene thumped a lump on her forehead before she was done.

Moonlily

(Mather AFB, California, 1956)

When we play horses at recess, my name
is Moonlily and I'm a yearling mare.
We gallop circles around the playground,
whinnying, neighing, and shaking our manes.
We scrape the ground with scuffed saddle oxfords,
thunder around the little kids on swings
and seesaws, and around the boys' ball games.
We're sorrel, chestnut, buckskin, pinto, gray,
a herd in pastel dresses and white socks.
We're self-named, untamed, untouched, unridden.
Our plains know no fences. We can smell spring.
The bell produces metamorphosis.
Still hot and flushed, we file back to our desks,
one bay in a room of palominos.

Cloud-Gathering

(Mather AFB, California, 1956)

Mama makes me close the book and go play.
Sometimes I join a pack of officers' kids
roaming the dry fields around Base Housing
and making traps for blue-bellied lizards.
Sometimes I lie among the cornflowers
and wild poppies, dreaming as clouds unfold:
Our baby has *the Mongolian spot* . . .
I'm glad they don't make me change his diapers . . .
White people down South want segregation . . .

They think brown is a contagious disease . . .
A mob attacked a girl for going to school . . .
I'd give anything to have a pony!
I'd call him Prince and feed him sugar cubes
and brush his mane and tail and ride bareback!

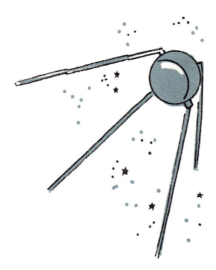

Sputnik

(Mather AFB, California 1957)

My Base School classmates play musical chairs:
sudden absences when dads get transferred,
friends who'll meet from now on only by chance.
Tonight might be the last slumber party
I'll giggle through with my best friend, Helene.
Tomorrow I'll feel lonely as *Sputnik*.
This girl in my class, Joanne, is pretty nice.
She invited me over after school.
But as soon as we got in her room, she closed the door,
opened the window, lit a cigarette,
and passed it to me. What's the point of that?
The grown-ups smoke: So what? I'd rather talk.
Helene talks about the kids in Little Rock:
how brave they are, how lonely they must feel.

Darkroom

(Mather AFB, California, 1957)

Tonight with Daddy in the dark bathroom,
I held my breath, watching science magic.
From white paper bathed in developer,
Jennifer and I on the piano bench
in a cloud of crisp, frothy crinolines
and other Easter finery emerged:
our hands in white gloves folded in our laps,
our patent Mary Janes and crossed anklets,
our temporary curling-iron curls.

After the stop bath and fixer, we hang
with clothespins on a line over the tub,
living colors reduced to black-and-white,
a lived moment captured in memory
Mama will put in the photo album.

Nelsons

Daddy's handsome: uniform, new haircut.
But the travel baby bed in our seat
crowds me and Jennifer. We kept asking,
"Are we there yet?" every few endless miles,
    until Daddy shouted, "HEY!" and braked. We braced
    ourselves. We skidded, turned, and spit gravel
    up a long driveway ending at a barn.
Barking dogs. Mama whispered Daddy's name.
A light-haired man came out. He calmed the dogs,
and looked at Daddy with inquiring eyes.
Daddy called, "Hello! We saw your mailbox!
We're Nelsons, too! I fly B-52s!
Would you mind letting my girls see your farm?"
That's why I'm here petting this stupid cow.

Fieldwork

(Portsmouth, New Hampshire, 1957)

Before he was sent to England for training,
Daddy said, "Let's pretend we're researching
an unknown civilian Caucasian tribe."
We live in a town apartment building
with shouting children clattering on the stairs.
For school lunch, they bring baked-bean sandwiches.
Some families eat for dinner only pie.
The sixth-grade boy next door is named Carrol;
his favorite lunch is onion on rye bread.
They say *tonic* for pop and *pock* for park.
They say our baby's *cunning*, meaning cute.
They say I look like Althea Gibson,
the First Negro to win the Wimbledon,
so I should start taking tennis lessons.

Caucasian Dinner

(Kittery Point, Maine, 1958)

Mama's rented a colonial house
a block from the ocean, in a village
where we're the First Negroes of everything.
We're the First Negro Family in Town,
the First Negro Children in the Town's School.
The Baylisses live in the house next door;
their mantel has photos of dead people
in their coffins. Uncle Ed sits all day
in their bay window with binoculars,
then comments on what we had for dinner.
Aunt Flossie asks us over for cookies.
Sometimes Mama lets me and Jennifer cook.
Tonight we made a Caucasian dinner:
cauliflower, broiled cod, mashed potatoes.

Ghost

(Kittery Point, Maine 1958)

This house in Kittery Point has felt like home
since the first night I slept in my own room,
furnished with bed, dresser, a vanity,
and framed art museum reproductions
of Renaissance paintings. It feels like home:
the first time I've felt like this in my life.
The deep front lawn perfect for badminton,
the wallpaper's somber floral designs,
the town library just across the street,
the Atlantic close enough to walk to:
It really feels like home. My one complaint
is that, on full-moon nights, a ghost appears.
She's hovering right now, near my closet,
daring me to call Jennifer again.

Attic Window

(Kittery Point, Maine, 1958)

Sweet Land of Liberty. Home of the Free.
The Melting Pot. The American Dream.
The Tooth Fairy. Adam and Eve. The Virgin Birth.
The more time I spend in the library,
the less sure I am about everything.
Did the Indians invite the Pilgrims
to their Thanksgiving feast? If so, I bet
the Pilgrims went home with the leftovers.
I read by the window in the attic,
and things people believe in are unmasked
like movie stars whose real names are revealed
in their obituaries. Jennifer
is such a baby, with her stuffed tiger
and that letter she's writing to Santa.

Paper Dolls

(Kittery Point, Maine, 1958)

I keep my area neatly policed
and always pass Saturday inspections.
You can't see the floor of Jennifer's room,
for all her clutter and her paper dolls.
I've heard her whispering voices for them,
tabbing on their cut-out paper outfits
and turning them into a puppet play.
She's too old to still be playing with dolls.
Besides, her mess drifts across the border
into my room, and she won't pick it up.
Today I took her stupid paper dolls
out to the burn-barrel in the backyard.
Daddy was burning documents and trash.
The flames rose in me as the dolls caught fire.

Queen of the Sixth Grade

(Kittery Point, Maine, 1958)

There was an accident in school today.
I shudder when I remember the crunch
of tibia and fibula and wood
as Jamie tried to get off the seesaw
and got her forearm accidentally
caught under her own weight and the up-kick
on the other end, increased by the force
Ellie and I used pushing her end down
so her seesaw seat slammed the blacktop hard
two or three times before she realized
what a mistake it was to say that name
she learned in some civilian school down South
before they got transferred and she came here
to this school, where I'm Queen of the Sixth Grade.

Aooga

(Kittery Point, Maine, 1958)

Visiting, Daddy found a Model T
buried under old furniture and junk
in Uncle Ed and Aunt Flossie's red barn,
in the meadow between their house and ours.
Uncle Ed said, "That cah's been dead for yee-ahs."
Daddy thought they might bring it back to life.
After several weekends of tinkering,
its sputter sparked into a miracle.
Now we chug off, Daddy behind the wheel,
on Sunday afternoon drives on back roads.
Uncle Ed and Aunt Flossie smile and wave
to neighbors generations intertwined.
Aunt Flossie wipes tears with her handkerchief.
Her veiny cheeks flush pink. Her white hair flows.

Beautiful Hair

(Kittery Point, Maine, 1958)

Second week of two at a summer camp
in the Maine woods somewhere, where there's a lake,
a lodge, sleeping cabins, and outhouses.
(The less you eat and drink, the less you go.)
I haven't seen Jennifer very much:
Our cabins are in different divisions.
I brought books, but there isn't time to read
because we're all so busy having fun.
My cabin-mates say they wish they were tan
like me. They say, "Your hair is beautiful;
can I touch it?" None of us understand
why integrating schools is a big deal.
When Mama and Daddy came on Parents' Day,
Mama screamed quietly, "My God! Your hair!"

Critic

(Kittery Point, Maine, 1959)

Daddy pulled a puppy from the pocket
of his flight jacket, and we imprinted
like a gosling to a goose. Speida's my dog,
though he's impartially affectionate.
Either he likes poems, or he likes my voice:
I read aloud from the anthology
I found with Daddy's other college books
and he sits, cocks his head, and wags his tail.
My teacher, Mrs. Gray, told me about
the famous poetess who lived near here.
She says I'll be a famous poet, too.
Today I read Speida one of my poems.
His face got a look of so much disgust
I laughed and forgot we're being transferred.

Parking Lot Dawn

(On the Road, 1959)

After the cousins came the long drive west.
Car games, sing-alongs, and conversation,
alternating drivers, meals in the car.
Gas station restrooms, or behind a tree.
Daddy corrects white men who call him boy.
Even when they're in police uniforms.
Even though the radio updates news
of sit-ins and white citizens' councils.

I ride behind his beautiful close-cropped head,
my window slightly cracked for Speida's nose.
Last night, awake alone, he parked the car
in the Grand Canyon visitors' parking lot.
And this morning, he woke us up to dawn.
There's more beauty on Earth than I can bear.

A Drift of Girlfriends

(Sacramento, California, 1959)

We've moved to a neighborhood of new homes
being built to be sold to Negro families.
Mama said she's proud we're landowners now,
like her papa was in Oklahoma,
his red dirt farm stretching fertile acres.
Daddy plowed our bare yard in the Lincoln,
breaking up the clods with its white-walled tires.
I walk to and from school, books to my chest,
with a drift of girlfriends, none of them mine.
I'm learning that Negro is a language
I don't speak. And I don't know how to dance.
At home, we listen to Miles and Coltrane,
Tchaikovsky and Chopin. I get good grades
because I'm curious and I like to read,
and NOT because I'm "trying to be white."

Africans

(Sacramento, California, 1959)

Mama brings Africans home from grad school,
like a kid who keeps finding lost puppies.
She's so proud of their new independence.
She brings home smooth-faced mahogany men,
dressed in suits like beautiful pajamas,
so Jennifer and I can shake their hands.
Nodding polite answers to her questions,
they go to town on her catfish and grits.
Later, while Daddy drives them to their dorms,
she washes and Jennifer and I dry.
"Some of the greatest wrongs of history
are being righted now," she says. "These are
our people." As I put a plate away,
I ask myself who is not my people.

Bitter Apple

(Sacramento, California, 1959)

Who should be transferred here but Helene's dad!
Miracle of miracles! Thank you, God!
Last night, the first of what we vow will be
many sleepovers, she explained to me
in whispers that excluded Jennifer
something she's learned since our last heart-to-heart
when we were stationed here two years ago:
how to get a boy's love, and how to kiss.
I don't know what she said: It's hard to hear
when someone's words are breath tickling your ear.
But what I understood has made me taste
the bitter apple of disappointment.
To think souls touching is so trivial
you can practice it with a Coke bottle.

The History of Tribal Suppression

(On the Road, 1959)

We drive through Indian territory,
every vista inhabited by ghosts
almost visible on the horizon.
Daddy says he has some Indian blood;
something he thinks his mother told him once.
Mama, as co-pilot, reads from the map
the history of tribal suppression.
Plump, brown-faced weavers sit along the road.
At last, Daddy pulls over. TRADING POST.
I choose a turquoise and silver bracelet;
Jennifer picks an authentic tom-tom.
Too many miles later to turn around,
she sees the tom-tom says "Made in Japan."
And my wrist is beginning to turn green.

Sinfonia Concertante

(Fort Worth, Texas, 1959)

Daddy's here on temporary duty,
so Mama's piano is in storage.
Home is a four-room third-floor apartment
in a Negro quarter of the city.
My all-black classmates act like I'm from Mars.
Are you the girl from California?
Talk for us. And these boys act like I'm cute!
Miss Jackson saw me pretend piano
and had me put into a music class.
String quartet: two violins, cello,
and on viola, me, sawing away.
Daddy says my squawks set his teeth on edge,
so I practice out on the balcony,
genius on view all up and down the block.

Mischievious

Between classes, teachers patrol the halls,
slapping their palms with short, thick leather straps.
Some tell kids to "assume the position,"
then whack them with perforated paddles.
My English teacher uses a ruler
to smack the palms of kids who mispronounce.
His bugbear's *mischievous,* which every kid
who reads it pronounces *mischievious.*
That added syllable drives the man mad.
He blew his stack when I corrected him:
"They're *eu-cal-YP-tus,* not *eu-CAL-yp-tus,* trees."
(I guess I was being *mischievious.*)
He said, "Stand up and hold out your right hand."
I'm in the office now. Mama's coming.

To Miss Jackson

(Fort Worth, Texas, 1959)

Miss Jackson loans me her own poetry books:
More Hughes, Cullen, Johnson. Gwendolyn Brooks,
First Negro Poet to Win the Pulitzer Prize.
(Maybe she's trying to tell me something.)
Isolated by temporariness
and unable to wholly comprehend
the things boys say to me under their breath
when we pass by each other in the hall
so close that we can sense each other's heat,
I flee into the arms of poetry.
I take my books to bed. I read so late
Daddy shouts, "Lights OUT!" Then Mama urges,
"Get the Man's hand out of your dad's pocket!"
I lie in the dark. My head whirls with words.

Let Me Count the Ways

(On the Road, 1959)

A sleeping princess startled from a dream
of tall, dark, handsome fifteen-year-old boys
surrounding me, like Gidget on the beach,
with warm eyes and begging-to-be-kissed lips,
cute, eager, willing . . . I'm back in my place
in the backseat, my face a fist because
I've been robbed of such tantalizing fruit.
Odessa's brother told her he likes me.
Now I won't find out if he's my true love.
I'm so bummed out. Life is passing me by.
Texas is becoming Oklahoma.
What if Odessa's brother was my prince?
How might I have loved him, given the chance?
I count the ways as miles and time streak past.

A Quartet of Geeks

(Clinton-Sherman AFB, Oklahoma, 1959)

All Hell seems to be breaking out down South!
My days start with radio news; they end
blessing the students integrating schools
and giving thanks for the National Guard.
Here, in God-Forsaken, Oklahoma,
we live on-base in the good neighborhood.
Majors and Colonels get bigger homes,
NCOs have an apartment complex.
We're assigned three bedrooms, two baths, garage.
There's no school on the base. We have to go
to schools in town: our teachers' First Negroes
(though I doubt they pronounce the word that way),
and the First Negroes of most of the kids.
But I've found a place in the seventh-grade cliques
with three best friends: We're a quartet of geeks.

Dances With Doorknobs

(Clinton-Sherman AFB, Oklahoma, 1959)

When Daddy's in control of the high-fi,
we listen to his favorite jazz albums.
Sometimes Mama talks about way back when
the greats were just young musicians on tour,
unwelcome in hotels. How this one stayed
with them once or twice, before I was born;
how that one loved her chicken and dumplings.
Sunday afternoons, Mama's in control
of which LP will release its music:
Marian Anderson, Mahler, Heifetz.
But I have a transistor radio,
the latest thing. One hand on the doorknob,
I jitterbug alone in our bedroom
when Jennifer's not here. Not often enough.

My Friends

(Clinton-Sherman AFB, Oklahoma, 1959)

My friends all live in the same neighborhood
because our dads are officers. We're stars
in all classes except gym, and, outside
of school, part of each other's families.
Cheryl dropped by last Saturday afternoon,
as Mama finished straightening our hair,
and said she smelled hair burning. Jennifer said,
"We put our heads in the oven once a week."
The other day at lunch, John blurted out,
"Your eyes aren't black, they're brown!" He'd just noticed
that he hadn't really been seeing me.
His mom talks to me as if we're equals.
Last night Kim, Cheryl, and I slept outside
in Kim's yard, giggling under the stars.

The Baby Picture Guessing Game

(Clinton-Sherman AFB, Oklahoma, 1959)

The Home Ec Baby Picture Guessing Game
ended soon for me: Everyone could see
which baby I was. They all looked alike.
When all the babies were identified,
they gave the Cutest Baby prize to me
and we ate the cupcakes we'd baked and iced.
My classmates voted down a class party
at the Elk City Theatre because
Negroes have to sit in the balcony.
Oh, it's not a bed of thornless roses:
Some of the farm boys punch each other's arms
and make kissy sounds when they walk past me.
But Mama and Daddy tell me every day
that I'm a cygnet in a flock of ducks.
And anyway, it isn't Little Rock.

Safe Path Through Quicksand

(Clinton-Sherman AFB, Oklahoma, 1959)

I belong to the Protestant Youth Group
and go to chapel on Sunday mornings.
Do I believe? Well, let's just say I hope.
I think Jesus is an elder brother
whose footsteps mark a safe path through quicksand.
Maybe we're already in "Heaven" now:
Every place I've been holds its own beauty.
But I do hope to God there is a hell
waiting for some people. For racist cops.
For grandmothers who spit hate at children.
A hell for mean, sneering, slicked-back-hair guys
like Rick Havard and Donald Goeringer.
A hell for Mr. and Mrs. Purdy,
who smile at me in class, and do evil.

How I Discovered Poetry

(Clinton-Sherman AFB, Oklahoma, 1959)

It was like soul-kissing, the way the words
filled my mouth as Mrs. Purdy read from her desk.
All the other kids zoned an hour ahead to 3:15,
but Mrs. Purdy and I wandered lonely as clouds borne
by a breeze off Mount Parnassus. She must have seen
the darkest eyes in the room brim: The next day
she gave me a poem she'd chosen especially for me
to read to the all-except-for-me white class.
She smiled when she told me to read it, smiled harder,
said oh yes I could. She smiled harder and harder
until I stood and opened my mouth to banjo-playing
darkies, pickaninnies, disses and dats. When I finished,
my classmates stared at the floor. We walked silent
to the buses, awed by the power of words.

Thirteen-Year-Old American Negro Girl

(Clinton-Sherman AFB, Oklahoma, 1959)

My face, as foreign to me as a mask,
allows people to believe they know me.
Thirteen-Year-Old American Negro Girl,
headlines would read if I was newsworthy.
But that's just the top-of-the-iceberg me.
I could spend hours searching the mirror
for clues to my truer identity,
if someone didn't pound the bathroom door.
You can't see what the mirror doesn't show:
for instance, that after I close my book
and turn off my lamp, I say to the dark:
Give me a message I can give the world.
Afraid there's a poet behind my face,
I beg until I've cried myself to sleep.

Author's Note

This book is a late-career retrospective, a personal memoir, a "portrait of the artist as a young American Negro Girl." The poems cover the decade of the fifties, from 1950, when I was four years old, to 1960, when I was fourteen.

I prefer to call the girl in the poems "the Speaker," not "me." Although the poems describe a girl whose life is very much like mine, the incidents the poems describe are not entirely or exactly "memories." They are sometimes much enhanced by research and imagination.

The Speaker's growing awareness of personal and racial identity are set against the tensions America experienced during the fifties. Some of the poems that seem to be "about me" are as much about the "Red Scare," the shadow of the atom bomb, racism, the rise of the Civil Rights Movement, or the first stirrings of women's empowerment.

Each of the poems is built around a "hole" or "gap" in the Speaker's understanding. As she grows older, the holes are less obviously evident, but they are always there. Her maturing voice, growing self-awareness, and broadening interests are a major theme of the book.

This is also the story of military family life. Though this is the specific story of the wife and children of one of the first African American career officers in the Air Force, most military families share some of the experiences described here. Their frequent transfers cause a sense of rootlessness, as the extended family and friends are more and more often seen waving good-bye as the family drives away. For most military children, home is something more longed for than known.

Another theme of the book is the Speaker's increasing fascination with language. In the last poem, at approximately the age of Confirmation or Bat Mitzvah, she realizes, with a feeling of awe and responsibility, that she may grow up to be a poet. As that poet, I have written this book as a sequence of fifty unrhymed sonnets. Like other sonnets, these have fourteen lines, and are roughly iambic pentameter (ten syllables per line), but they don't rhyme, and they don't always have the traditional volta, or "turn" from one thought to another thought, in the middle.

I'd like to thank my sister, Jennifer Nelson, for helping me remember things; and to thank my friends Inge Pedersen and Stephen Roxburg for giving me good advice; and to thank my editor, Lauri Hornik, for pushing me to develop my original idea; and to thank my agent, Regina

Brooks of Serendipity Literary Agency, for cheering me on; and to thank my friend Pamela Espeland for thinking through things with me and making me laugh as I worked on the poems.

Who's Who in the family photos:

page 46, left: Marilyn's mama and daddy, Johnnie and Melvin
Nelson, Melvin's aunts Edith and Effie, Marilyn, and younger sister
Jennifer; right: Marilyn, Mama, and Jennifer in the Painted Desert

page 47: Marilyn and Jennifer on the Pacific coast

back cover: Marilyn's parents, Lt. Melvin Nelson and Johnnie
Mitchell Nelson, newlyweds

The author gratefully acknowledges the editors
of the following publications, in which some
of these poems first appeared:

Fields of Praise: New and Selected Poems by Marilyn Nelson,
copyright 1994, 1995, 1996, 1997, Louisiana State University
Press: "How I Discovered Poetry"

Beloit Poetry Journal (Vol. 62, No. 3, Spring 2012) *Split This Rock
Chapbook 2012:* "Called Up," "Your Own," "Making History"

"30 Poets/30 Days: April 2012," GottaBook blog (gottabook.
blogspot.com): "Telling Time"

Tygerburning Literary Journal (No. 2, Summer 2013): "Pink
Menace," "Mississippi"

Saranac Review (No. 8, 2013–2014): "Career Girl"

Cimarron Review (No. 180, Summer 2012): "Nelsons," "Parking
Lot Dawn," "Thirteen-Year-Old American Negro Girl"